"I have so much admiration for this kid. Tiger is one of my idols. I am in awe of what he's done."

— *Michael Jordan*

18 HOLES WITH

TIGER

By the Staff of Beckett Publications

Cover Photo By Al Messerschmidt

ROBERT BECK

Contents

"He may be the type of player who
comes along once a millennium."
— *Tom Watson on Tiger Woods*

Front Nine: *The Player*

6	1ST HOLE	THE PHENOMENON
14	2ND HOLE	THE CHILD PRODIGY
22	3RD HOLE	THE PARENTS
30	4TH HOLE	THE MASTERS
38	5TH HOLE	THE STUDENT
46	6TH HOLE	THE MOTIVATOR
54	7TH HOLE	THE CORPORATION
62	8TH HOLE	THE ROLE MODEL
70	9TH HOLE	THE CELEBRITY

Back Nine: *The Game*

78	10TH HOLE	THE AMATEUR
86	11TH HOLE	THE PRO
94	12TH HOLE	THE SWING
100	13TH HOLE	THE POWER
106	14TH HOLE	THE ARTIST
112	15TH HOLE	THE PUTTER
120	16TH HOLE	THE COURSE
128	17TH HOLE	THE LOOK
136	18TH HOLE	THE COMPARISONS

"What Michael Jordan did for basketball, [Tiger Woods] absolutely can do for golf."
— *Phil Knight, Nike CEO*

On Aug. 28, 1996, the world changed. The year before Tiger Woods joined the Professional Golfers of America Tour, his claim to fame was limited to the links. From the age of 3 Tiger had made news as a young golf prodigy. As a teenager, Tiger had claimed a roomful of

On Aug. 28, 1996, Tiger announced his intention to take a shot at the PGA Tour and golf world as a professional. A record gallery turned out at the Greater Milwaukee Open to witness Tiger's pro debut.

amateur trophies. Less than a year later, Tiger trailed only Michael Jordan as the most recognized product endorser.

His name, likeness, words and actions have caught the eye of golfers and non-golfers alike. Inner-city kids have put down their basketballs and picked up their first bag and clubs. Teenagers, both male and female

THE PHENOMENON

Tiger's phenomenal success as an amateur drew the eyes of the world to his first pro tournament where he finished 60th. Tiger claimed his first PGA title a month later in Las Vegas.

Whether it's across fairways or along cart paths, cameramen and other media-types are always close behind Tiger Woods, not wanting to miss a shot of golf's answer to Michael Jordan.

have been inspired to take to the course and take their first swings at a sport they can enjoy

for a lifetime. Spectators flock to the tournaments and wait along the ropes for their chance

to witness a moment of history. Longtime golfers have glimpsed the emergence of the

world's next dominant professional golfer.

The attraction to Tiger is the same. People of all ages, races and walks of life have identified with the 21-year-old phenomenon named Tiger Woods.

"I want to be the next dominant player."

— *Tiger Woods, age 14*

Tiger experienced his first inspira-
tion to pick up a golf club before
his first birthday while watching his
father, Earl, practice. The pair
proved to be inseparable during
Tiger's meteoric ascension through
the junior golf circuits.

Tiger Woods learned to swing a golf club before he could walk.

When he was 6 months old, he sat in his high chair and watched his father, Earl, practice his swing. At 10 months, Tiger was hitting balls into a practice net using a club shortened by his father. At 18 months, the toddler could hit golf balls on the driving range beside Earl. When he grew tired, his mother, Kultida, would plop Tiger back into the stroller for a bottle and a nap. **At age 3,** Tiger shot 48 for nine holes and appeared on every major television network, including a putting contest with comedian Bob Hope. **At age 4,** Tiger carried his own golf bag and played in his

Tiger's record-breaking junior golf
triumphs against his peers and
even competition beyond his years
produced a family scrapbook of
victory snapshots.

THE CHILD PRODIGY

first tournament. At age 5, Tiger displayed his swing on the TV show *That's Incredible.* At age 8 he was shooting in the 70s. By the age of 13, Tiger already had tallied five holes-in-one and had played an exhibition against golf legend Sam

Snead. At age 14, Tiger's mugshot appeared in *Sports Illustrated's* "Faces in the Crowd." At 16 years, 2 months, Tiger was invited to play in the Los Angeles Open, making him the youngest player ever to compete in a PGA event.

"They have raised me well, and I truly believe they have taught me to accept full responsibility for all aspects of my life."

— *Tiger Woods*

L ieutenant Colonel Earl Woods and his wife, Kultida, met while working together in the U.S. Army office in Bangkok in 1967. **On Dec. 30, 1975, Tida gave birth to Eldrick Woods** in Long Beach, Calif. Earl soon would hang the moniker "Tiger" on his son, in memory of a South Vietnamese army buddy he had dubbed "Tiger" for his bravery.

From youth tournaments to professional golf's majors, Tida and Earl Woods, also known as Team Tiger, have followed their son around the globe to help Tiger realize his goal of being the best golfer of all time.

In 1996, the year Tiger went professional at the age of 20, Earl was 64. Tida was 52.

Before that historic announcement, Tiger's parents had devoted their lives to their only son.

Earl was the teacher.

He fine-tuned Tiger's swing and his mind, both encouraging and challenging the young prodigy. His attention to Tiger was constant and unconditional, but he pushed his son's abilities and potential. Earl often tested Tiger's concentration by jingling coins or coughing during his swing.

Earl Woods participates in youth clinics sponsored by the Tiger Woods Foundation. The clinics allow the father and son to promote youth golf programs and to pass on life lessons on subjects such as setting goals, parental support and drug abuse.

Tida nurtured Tiger's emotions and heart.

She walked the thousands of holes her son played as a junior golfer and introduced him to the study of Buddhism.

Today the Woods' son is a multimillionaire and considered to be the best player in the world. But Earl and Tida still play the loving and supportive roles that helped Tiger become the best he could be in golf and in life.

"Arnold [Palmer] and I agree that you could take his Masters and my Masters and add them together, and this kid should win more than that." —*Jack Nicklaus*

The images of Tiger's land-mark triumph at the 1997 Masters unwind in rapid-fire succession.

Chipping in for birdie from behind the green at the

par-3 12th on Thursday, which sparked a sizzling six-under 30 on the back nine. Hitting second-shot wedges to the 500-yard par-5 15th. Driving the gallery crosswalk on the par-4 17th. Flashing his million-dollar smile on Saturday after hitting a sand wedge to within a foot of the 18th hole to cap a seven-under 65.

By Sunday afternoon the numbers told the story at the 1997 Masters. No one would keep Tiger from putting his victory trademark on the historic accomplishment on the 18th green at Augusta National.

Unleashing his patented victory punch Sunday on the 18th after sinking a 5-foot putt to finish 18 under par, one of many tournament records. Hugging Lee Elder, the first black man to play in the Masters.

STEVE MUNDAY / ALLSPORT USA

Accepting the green jacket (42-long) from Nick Faldo as the first black man to conquer Augusta National. In becoming the youngest Masters winner (Seve Ballesteros won it at age 23 in 1980), 21-year-old Tiger brought the vaunted Augusta National course to its knees.

Tiger's "lucky" red Nike shirt made an impressive fashion statement beneath the coveted green jacket presented to him by defending Masters champion Nick Faldo.

His record-low, 72-hole score
of 270 gave him the championship by 12 strokes, the widest margin of victory

since Jack Nicklaus won the 1965 title by nine shots. Perhaps Jack was right.

"I saw a kid who popped out of the womb a Magic Johnson or a Mozart. [Tiger] had talent oozing out of his fingertips."

— Rudy Duran, Tiger's childhood golf coach

Earl and Tida Woods nurtured their son through his earliest years, but Tiger has reached out to other teachers in his pursuit of perfection.

At the most important junctures in his life, Tiger and his parents have managed to align him with the right guide at the best time.

Tiger's first instructor, Rudy Duran, spent more time on the practice range admiring his gifted student's swing than refining it. Current swing guru Butch Harmon, who began polishing the prodigy's stroke in 1994, takes a more hands-on approach.

At age 4, Earl turned Tiger over to Rudy Duran, the head pro at Heartwell Golf Park in Long Beach, Calif. Duran, a former PGA Tour player, gave Tiger another perspective on the technical elements of his swing. **When Tiger was 10,** Duran relocated, so Earl sought the help of John Anselmo, head teaching pro at Meadowlark Golf Course in Huntington Beach, Calif. Anselmo continued to **refine Tiger's swing and taught him the art of shotmaking through his high school years.**

RICHARD DOLE (3)

At age 14,

Tiger and his parents enlisted San Diego-based sports

psychologist Jay Brunza to refine the boy's already

brilliant mental game into a winning edge. Br

teaching techniques included hypnotism and

on-the-course training as a caddy for Tiger.

Tiger's talents took him to tournaments across the globe, but he still found time to attend Cypress Western High School and play with the school's golf

team under coach Don Crosby. As a freshman, Tiger was medalist in 27 of the team's 29 tournaments. Tiger graduated with the Class of '93.

Virtually every element of Tiger's golf swing can be traced to the teachings of father Earl, swing doctor Butch Harmon and instructor No. 2, John Anselmo.

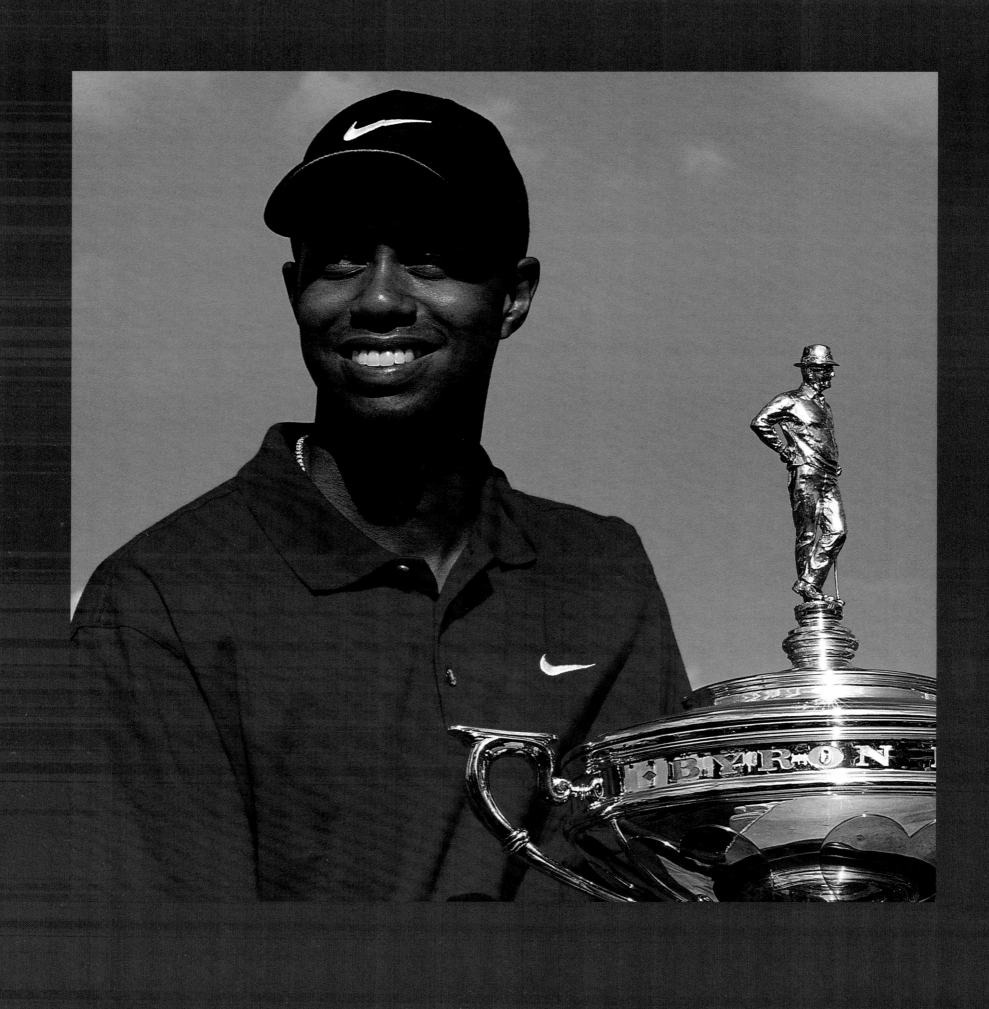

"He has this attitude where he wants to win every tournament. You have to learn to beat people's butts. Tiger has proven that he can do that." — *Tom Watson*

he media question him of his expectations at every tour stop. And Tiger's

answer is always the same. He expects to win every tournament he enters. If

not, why should he bother going through the motions?

As a youngster, Tiger grew motivated by his burgeoning talent and his drive to improve his golf game. That drive fed on inner strength and discipline and occasionally was fueled by conflicts of race and age.

Tiger's fierce competitive desire became a part of his game at an early age and continues to grow. In winning a record three straight U.S. Amateur titles, Tiger used his "edge" to conquer match-play opponents.

Today, Tiger has proven himself a champion at the highest level of his profession, but the inner fire has not been dimmed by success.

Tiger's celebratory displays can put an end to a hopeful opponent's chances or announce the looming presence of the golf predator. Tiger's fist puts an emotional exclamation point on great shots, championship rounds and personal triumph.

The biggest test of Tiger's brief career may have been his first round at the 1997 Masters. Four bogeys on the front nine, including holes 8 and 9, left Tiger at 4-over par at the turn. A huge gallery followed Tiger and defending Masters champion Nick Faldo to the 10th tee, where Tiger looked inside himself and took his first step toward the biggest victory in his young life. Tiger looked down the tight fairway and smashed a

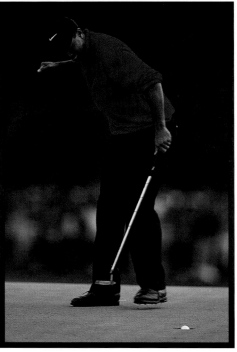

2-iron and then an 8-iron to within 10 feet and sank his putt

for a birdie on the longest par-4 at Augusta. Tiger would go

21-under for the remaining 62 holes.

"[Tiger] could have the most profound impact both inside and outside of sports of any athlete since Muhammad Ali."

— *Leigh Steinberg, sports agent*

The irony couldn't be ignored. Tiger's decision to turn pro at the Greater Milwaukee Open and his chance to play the remaining 1996 PGA events were based on sponsor exemptions. To gain his 1997 tour card, Tiger would have to finish in the top 125 moneymakers or face going to the PGA Qualifying School in the off-season. After finishing tied for 60th at Milwaukee, Tiger ranked 344th on the list. He'd won just a couple thousand dollars in the PGA's eyes, but **he'd already pocketed millions thanks to his marketability.**

When Tiger pondered the idea of turning pro, one sports apparel company's endorsement offer told him, "Just Do It."

From every angle, Tiger's golf apparel and equipment leave no doubt with whom his corporate allegiances lie. Endorsement deals with Nike and Titleist made Tiger a multimillionaire before he hit his first drive as a pro.

Companies were chomping at the bit for Tiger to turn pro, and who could blame him when the first two endorsement deals were placed on the table. A contract with Nike for $40 million.

An equipment deal from Titleist/Cobra worth $20 million.

To manage the corporate demands that came with his fame and fortune, **Tiger assembled his own Team Tiger.** Earl and Tida Woods head the team of decision-makers that includes the powerful International Management Group (IMG).

In less than a year on the PGA Tour, Tiger had risen to No. 5 on the list of athletes'

annual endorsement earnings behind Andre Agassi, Arnold Palmer, Shaquille O'Neal and list leader Michael Jordan. It's no surprise that at the 1997 U.S. Open, Team Tiger and Nike announced that, like Mike, Tiger would have his own apparel logo.

Rain or shine, Tiger's endorsements of Nike and Titleist put their stamp on a lucrative marketing future for golf's most recognizable name.

"I like the idea of being a role model. It's an honor. People took the time to help me as a kid, and they impacted my life. I want to do the same for kids." — *Tiger Woods*

As the youngest millionaire on the PGA Tour, Tiger stands as a role model for millions of young golfers throughout the United States. As part African-American, Caucasian, Cherokee, Chinese and Thai, Tiger's exposure also has transformed him into a role model for the world. His mother, Tida, has called him a universal child, and it is the children whom Tiger has chosen to lead.

While raising Tiger, Tida made it a point to expose her son to many universal cultures and philosophies. As a role model for children, Tiger has passed on his parents' lessons and his own beliefs.

Tiger's youth golf clinics provide children a personal look at how the young champion handles himself and his clubs. Tiger's youthful presence helps him get his message across.

ROBERT BECK

In 1997, Tiger and his parents formed the Tiger Woods Foundation for the purpose of promoting golf and other benefits for inner-city youths. The foundation draws its funding from Tiger and his marketing sponsors to reach out to thousands of children each year. The foundation's first campaign included a series of youth golf clinics coinciding with stops on the PGA Tour.

Hundreds of children are invited to attend each clinic, at which Tiger provides tips for their golf games and advice for their futures. The participants watch wide-eyed as Tiger booms 300-plus-yard drives and even shows off with some trick shots. They listen intently as Tiger delivers a message that urges them to stay in school and steer clear of drugs. His ever-present father does his part of the program by speaking to the children's parents.

What better role model can there be than the role model's model?

"It was like he was the Pope." — *Tida Woods*

"He's not the Pope. More like a god." — *Jack Nicklaus*

W hether it's President Clinton calling from the White House or a teen-age girl swooning over the most famous 21-year-old on the planet, Tiger Woods is looked upon as royalty.

Even the former Duchess of York, Sarah Ferguson, showed up to sit beside Tida and watch Tiger win the Byron Nelson Classic.

As the most sought-after celebrity
pro-am draw, Tiger has attracted
celebrity partners such as Kevin
Costner, baseball Hall of Famer
Reggie Jackson and television
journalist Bryant Gumbel.

When you're hot, you're hot, and Tiger

unofficially ranks as the superstar most superstars will do anything to meet. Tiger's recent

list of fans is long and very distinguished.

Movie star Kevin Costner teamed up with the tour's new drawing card at the Pebble

Beach pro-am.

Nearby Orlando neighbor Ken Griffey Jr. couldn't wait to tee it up with Tiger. And some 15-handicapper named Michael Jordan refers to Tiger as his idol.

Supermodel/Actress Cindy Crawford sent Tiger a letter of congratulations and a hint that a certain watch company would like to sign him to an endorsement deal.

But beyond the glitz and glamour that now circle around Tiger remain the everyday people who cheer him on from the galleries. It's longtime golf fans and newcomers drawn by the phenomenon who come out in record numbers to catch a glimpse of Tiger.

"What does it take to beat this guy? Only God knows." — *Steve Scott, Tiger's sudden-death victim in the final of the 1996 U.S. Amateur*

A

ll things short of divine intervention fell prey to the prodigy during his amateur career, a reign of other-worldly domination that began at age 8 with the Optimist International Junior World title and ended at 20 with the 38-hole shell-shocking of Scott at Pumpkin Ridge Golf Course in Cornelius, Ore.

Tiger came up short in just three of 45 USGA match-play contests: Dennis Hillman, '90 Junior Amateur; Tim Herron, '92 Amateur; and Paul Page, '93 Amateur.

His crowning achievements came in USGA national match-play championships, in which he compiled a 42-3 record. From 1991 through '96, Tiger proved unbeatable in 36 consecutive matches to win six straight titles: three Junior Amateurs and three Amateurs. No man — or golfing god such as Bobby Jones (five Amateur titles) and Jack Nicklaus (two) — had ruled three consecutive years.

Tiger bagged a bear in 1996 by becoming just the second golfer since Jack Nicklaus in 1961 to win the NCAA and Amateur titles in the same year (Phil Mickelson, 1991, was the first).

Other precedents came before Pumpkin Ridge: at 15, Tiger was the youngest Junior champ; at 16, he was the youngest entrant in a PGA Tour event; and at 18, he was the youngest player to win the Amateur.

None of Tiger's six USGA national titles was a walk in the park. He trailed in every final and survived sudden death three times, including the 38-hole thriller with Steve Scott in 1996.

After Amateur No. 1 at the TPC-Sawgrass Stadium Course, Tiger entered Stanford, a goal of his since junior high, evidenced by a letter expressing interest in the prestigious private school that he wrote to Cardinal golf coach Wally Goodwin.

As a freshman, he placed fifth in the NCAA Championships. The next year he triumphed. A few months later he polished off his Amateur trifecta, leaving him nothing humanly possible to prove on the amateur level.

"Hello, World. . . . I'm told I'm not ready for you. Are you ready for me?" — *brand-new pro Tiger Woods in Nike TV advertisement*

The Stanford sophomore joined elite company by trading his Cardinal cap for a logo-clad lid. Other collegians to leave school early include Fred Couples, Jack Nicklaus and Arnold Palmer.

N o one knew quite what to expect from the brash 20-year-old when on Aug. 28, 1996 – three days after his third Amateur triumph – he announced

his decision to turn pro.

The entire world, it seemed, had heard about his $60 million in endorsement deals with

Nike and Titleist. That enormous figure couldn't buy him a PGA Tour card, something he had

to earn in the next eight tournaments by finishing in the top 125 in tour earnings. Some

tour pros were skeptical.

"All those Amateur championships aren't going to scare anyone,"

11-year veteran Scott Verplank said.

On Aug. 29, Tiger played his first round as a pro, shooting 67 in the Greater Milwaukee Open. He would finish tied for 60th, good for $2,544. No one was shaking in his cleats — despite shots such as his first drive, a 335-yard coming-out projectile down the middle of the fairway.

THE PRO

No one, not even the young man who expects to win every tournament he enters, could have predicted that in 12 months on tour Tiger would win six events, a major title and in excess of $2.5 million.

A month later the Tiger dropped another bomb.

He beat Davis Love III in a playoff for the $297,000 first-place check at the Las Vegas Invitational. Two weeks later Tiger trimmed Payne Stewart by a shot to win the Walt Disney World/Oldsmobile Classic. He wound up cashing $790,594 in checks to finish 24th in earnings. He had his card, yet even then, no one was prepared for what would transpire during four days in April 1997 on the pristine grounds of a former tree nursery in Augusta, Ga.

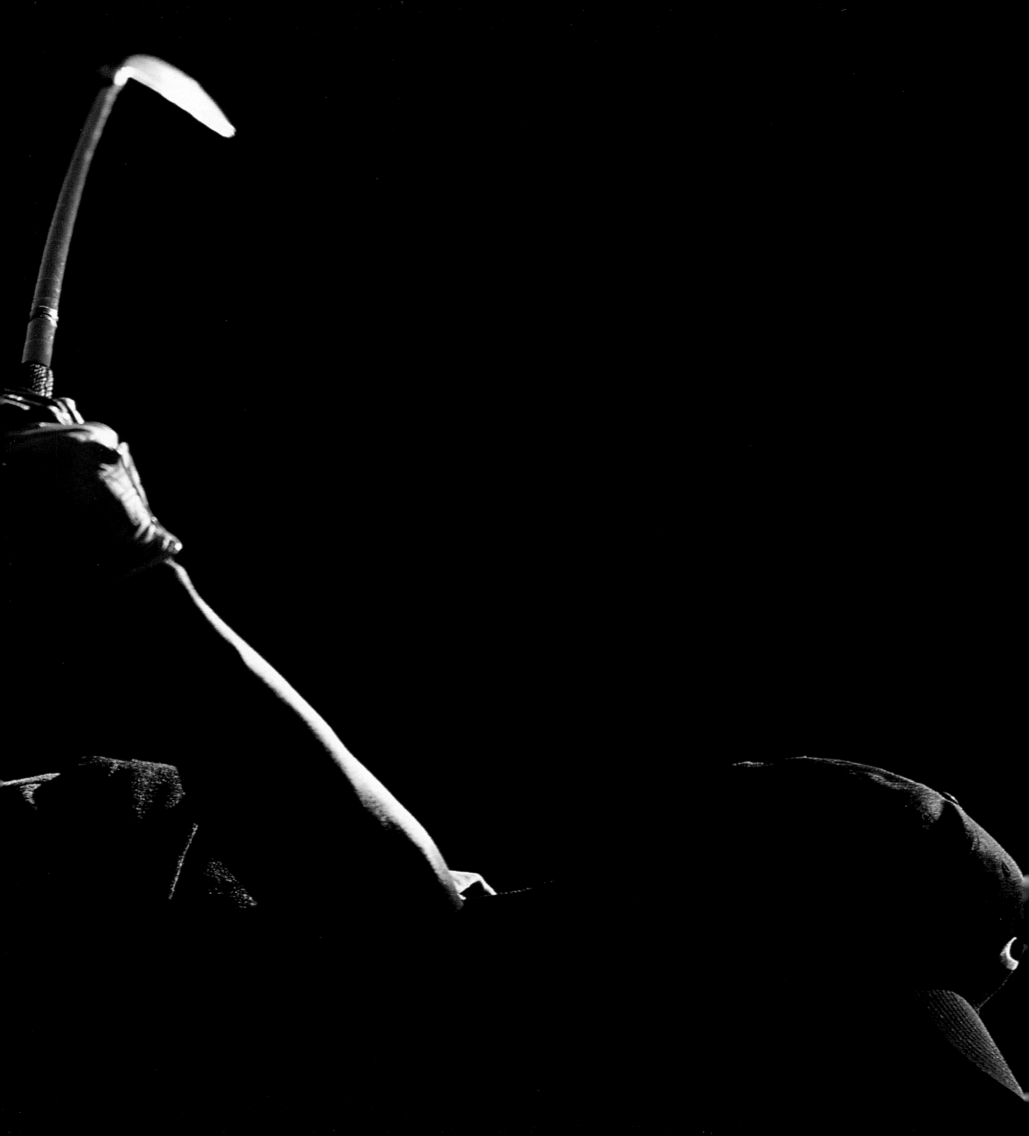

"[A pretty swing doesn't] break down into parts any more than a wonderful poem breaks down into words." — Harvey Penick in his *Little Red Book*

When you watch Tiger attack the ball, the first words that spring to mind probably aren't "pretty" or "beautiful" or "graceful." The late, great Mr. Penick was waxing poetic about the smooth-as-molasses stroke of Scotsman MacDonald Smith, a member of the PGA Hall of Fame. Just as easily, Mr. Penick could have been talking about current sweet swingers such as pros Payne Stewart and Ernie Els, or women counterparts Beth Daniel and Kelly Robbins.

Tiger doesn't qualify, at least not in the classic sense. "Pretty," in Tiger's case, lies in efficiency and exactness of movement. His stroke inspires "ooos" and "ahhhs" as if it were a shiny, blue-steel Smith & Wesson. Factor in the resulting awesome power, and Tiger's pass at the ball borders on the brutally efficient.

Two greats, NBC analyst Johnny Miller and the Golden Bear, Nicklaus, call it the

most technically efficient swing they've ever seen.

The young man in question simply calls on it to produce beautiful results.

"He's so long, he reduces the course to nothing, absolutely nothing."
— *six-time Masters winner Jack Nicklaus on Tiger's mauling of Augusta National*

Babe Ruth single-handedly revolutionized baseball with his irresistible combination of charisma and home run power. The Babe shattered the major league record for home runs with 29 in 1919, then whipped fans into a frenzy the next year with 54 — more that year than every other team.

Golf's answer to the home run is the **300-yard drive** — virtually all carry and straight down the middle of the fairway.

Tiger, all 6-2, 155 pounds of him, has bombed more of those

than any other tour pro in 1997 and will do so well into the 21st century. Nine rounds short of qualifying for the '96 tour rankings, he averaged 302.8 yards per drive, 4 yards longer than longest hitter John Daly. In 1997, Tiger led wire-to-wire to become the official distance champ.

Since the PGA Tour measures drives on just two holes at tournaments, Tiger's "average" doesn't do justice to his Ruthian power. The only exception occurred during his landmark victory at the 1997 Masters, in which

Players report gaining 20 to 30 yards by switching to graphite-shafted Titanium drivers. Tiger, who tried graphite as a teenager, clings faithfully to a steel-shafted Cobra driver designed for control, not distance.

Tiger posted a 323-yard average, 25 yards more than the next

longest golfer.

Other prodigious feats already have entered the realm of long-ball legend. No. 1: Parting

a stiff, heavy ocean breeze with two monstrous wood shots to reach the famous

548-yard par-5 18th at Pebble Beach during the final round of the 1997 AT&T

National Pro Am. No. 2: Becoming just the second player ever to require just two bombs to

hit the 569-yard par-5 17th at the LaCosta Resort in the '97 Mercedes Championships.

"I've learned to trust the subconscious. My instincts have never lied to me." — *Tiger Woods*

G olf instructors seldom agree on anything, but they do see eye-to-eye on at least one subject: **visualizing your shot.**

Before address, they advise, stand behind the ball and imagine its preferred flight.

See it fading or drawing and landing on the green or in the fairway.

Their words are wasted on Tiger Woods.

He takes his pre-shot routine a step further,

or more accurately, a step deeper. Tiger's

imagination leaves too much to chance. If he

merely visualizes a high, soft faded 9-iron

over water to a tight pin placement, he might

impart so much spin on the ball that it hits

the green and sucks back into the water.

Rather, he feels the shot that will produce the optimum results. Like a sculptor, Tiger approaches each shot as if it were a rough block of granite. He takes in everything — wind, obstacles, hazards, lie, target (green or fairway) — **and lets the shape of the shot reveal itself.** He doesn't see the result in his mind's eye; he feels it in his arms, legs and torso. The actual swing conforms itself to those sensations.

Swinging the same Mizuno forged irons he started using in high school, Tiger prefers a subtle right-to-left ball flight, but he has learned to let the conditions shape his shots: left-to-right skyscrapers, knocked-down draws and fades, low burners below and between trees, and so on.

If conditions call for a three-quarter 7-iron with a slight draw, he'll stand behind the ball feeling his weight concentrated on his left foot, a firm, easy, abbreviated backswing and a rolling of the wrists through impact, the clubface low and along the target line. For a 330-yard drive, the upper body coils tightly, then unwinds with a violent firing of the right shoulder and hip.

No shot feels the same, but virtually every one looks like a work of art.

"Everybody has been waiting for another Jack [Nicklaus], a guy who can hit it farther than anybody else and can putt. Perhaps he's here."
— *Jay Haas, tour veteran*

Y ou have your great putters and your great clutch putters. At this stage of his career, Tiger Woods falls closer to the latter category.

Though capable of hot streaks with the short stick, he's no "Boss of the Moss," no smooth-as-butter putter cut from the mold of a Ben Crenshaw, who rolled to two Masters titles with "Little Ben," the most famous putter since Bobby Jones' "Calamity Jane."

The mark of a great putter doesn't lie in making 30-footers, but in converting 5- to 8-footers for birdie or par. Tiger showed flashes of greatness at the '97 Masters by not three-putting, but three three-jacks in the third round of the U.S. Open caused him to fall to 19th place.

ROBERT BECK

Tiger, also, is no Nicklaus, who isn't considered a great roller of the ball but is hailed as the best pressure putter ever. If you could pick anyone to putt a 10-footer to win a major, you'd pick the Golden Bear, the all-time leader with 20 major titles. Or, you'd lose to the person who picked Jack.

That may not be the case in the near future if Tiger keeps it up. He's already filled a small bucket with balls that rattled the bottom of the cup during the height of competitive heat.

Who can forget Tiger's 15-foot knockout of Trip Kuehne on the island 17th at TPC-Sawgrass in the final of the '94 U.S. Amateur? Or the 30-foot drain work on the 35th hole of

Players choose either to charge the hole and risk lip-outs, or to let the ball die in the hole and risk coming up short. Tiger subscribes to the make-or-break approach, while "Gentle" Ben Crenshaw follows the philosophy of live and let die.

the '96 Amateur to complete a five-stroke comeback and set up the sudden-death

victory?

Then came his 1997 Masters triumph and nary a three-putt on greens just a notch

slower than the polished hood of a '57 Chevy.

His flair for the dramatic resurfaced at the '97

British Open when he canned a

par-saving 10-footer to seal his course

record-tying 64 and put a scare into the

front-runners.

Tiger would fade on Sunday, but his

final stroke the day before will endure as

one in a long line of memorable putts.

"I won with my mind this week."

— Tiger Woods, after winning the 1997 Motorola Western Open

I t wasn't the first time Tiger relied on his mind more than his might to defeat his primary opponent — the course.

The world's most famous 21-year-old leveled the playing field at the 1997 Masters with his laser-straight 330-yard drives. Yet he didn't fire an 18-under total of 270 on the strength of extraordinary length alone.

Playing many courses for the first time in 1996 and '97, Tiger received yardages and local knowledge from 20-year tour caddie Mike "Fluff" Cowan, who joined Team Tiger with the blessings of former boss Peter Jacobsen.

Tiger Woods set the tournament record with his brains, not his brawn.

To prepare for his first major as a pro, the Orlando, Fla., resident would go to The Golf Channel at night and study footage of select Masters. With the help of veteran caddie Mike "Fluff" Cowan, Tiger beat the course by teeing off with a 3-wood or 2-iron when position outranked distance (it helps to hit a 3-wood 300 yards) and leaving himself with level or uphill putts on the driveway-fast greens. In shooting a 7-under 65 on Saturday, he missed only one fairway and one green. Before the deluge, Nick Faldo and Steve Elkington said it takes several years playing and learning Augusta National to have a chance to master it. In Tiger's unfathomable wake, Tom Kite said the 21-year-old champ played with the wisdom of a pro of 30. Other conquests followed: Tiger's winning of the GTE Byron Nelson with his "C-plus game" and his A-plus course management; then two months later his thought-provoking final -round 68 to break a three-way tie for first and win the Western by three over Frank Nobilo.

didn't beat him; his balky putter in the rain-delayed third round dropped him from contention.

ROBERT BECK

ROBERT BECK

Tiger knew he had the game and mind to navigate the hazards of professional golf well before he dusted Steve Scott in sudden death at Pumpkin Ridge Golf Club to complete the historic U.S. Amateur triple. It wouldn't be long before the world knew, too.

It was his fourth victory of 1997, pushing his earnings to $1,761,033, less than $20,000 short of Tom Lehman's single-season tour record. **Mind-boggling.**

"I can get into that totally obsessed state. . . . I know how to focus. I've done it before." — *Tiger Woods*

Wbhen it boils down to one-on-one confrontations, Tiger Woods is to golf what Michael Jordan is to basketball. Both rise to their best at crunch time – when they sense victory.

Like Jordan hitting a game-winning jump shot, Tiger seizes the heated
moment with searing drives, pin-seeking iron shots
and center-cut putts. If the first doesn't slay his prey, the second or
third will.

Jordan's pressure-packed conquests are legion; Tiger's are becoming so:

• three U.S. Amateur finals victories, two of which he roared back from five strokes down in the final 18;

• sudden-death PGA Tour triumphs at the 1996 Las Vegas Invitational (Davis Love III) and '97 Mercedes Championships (Tom Lehman);

• final-round 66 to clip playing partner Payne Stewart by one at the '96 Walt Disney/Oldsmobile Classic;

• last-round 68s to claim the '97 Byron Nelson and Western Open tour stops;

• humbling playing partners Nick Faldo and Colin Montgomerie in his '97 Masters massacre.

You don't have to look at the leaderboard to know when Tiger's in the hunt. One glance at him tells it all: his confident stride, the pump of a fist, and the eyes — like those of a hawk at hunt.

It's the Look that thrills us. Before Tiger, Ben Hogan perfected it. Ray Floyd practiced it. Jack Nicklaus immortalized it.

Now, Tiger — like Mike — has it at his command.

"Woods is a combination of Jack Nicklaus and Arnold Palmer. His tremendous star quality makes him bigger than life." — *Tim Finchem, PGA Tour commissioner*

We've shuddered at the roar of Bear Apparents before.

Jerry Pate and Hal Sutton lost the tag as "The Next Nicklaus" as quickly as they earned

it. Then the unbearable weight tumbled from the wide shoulders of John Daly and Phil

Mickelson — Daly because of uncontrolled fury on and off the course and Mickelson because

of greatness unsustained.

Tiger fits into history's enormous bear tracks much more comfortably than the fearsome foursome before him. He hits it farther than anyone on tour (as

Nicklaus did in the 1960s and '70s), he won his first green jacket at 21 (Jack won three of six Masters by 26), and Tiger has an uncanny ability to sink putts when drama is at its height (as did Nicklaus regularly).

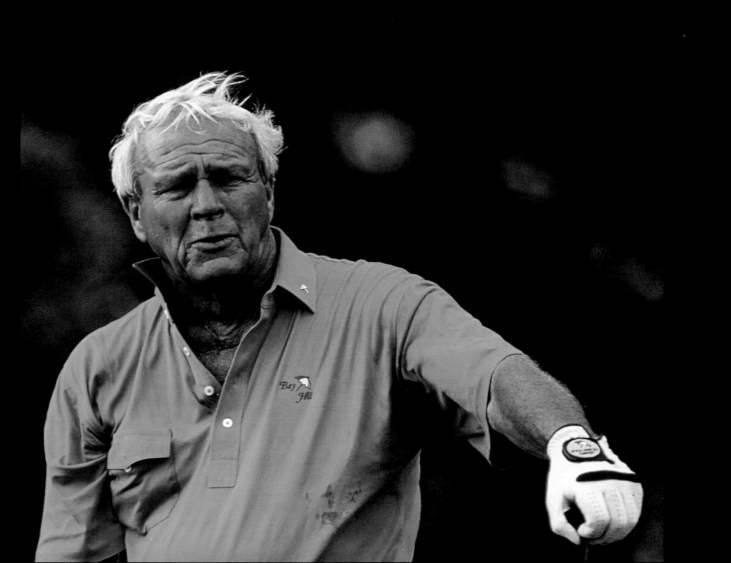

The King is dead; long live the King. Before Tiger, no one dared label a player as the next Arnold Palmer and Jack Nicklaus rolled into one. For Phil Mickelson, it's hard enough being the latest in a long line of phenoms branded the next Golden Bear.

His own young man, Tiger can't be trapped by single-player comparisons. The game hasn't seen such drawing power since the reign of the King, Arnold Palmer, the baggy-panted swashbuckler who single-handedly triggered golf's first boom in the '60s. **Arnie's Army has been replaced by Tigermania,** a media-fueled phenomenon gripping people of all ages and races and elevating tournament attendance and TV ratings to unseen levels.

The wonder that is Woods shares traits with two other greats: Seve Ballesteros and his imaginative out-of-troubleshooting, and Tom Watson's bold iron play and aggressive putting style. Other comparisons abound, each because their diversity brings us back to where we

"Tiger could end up like Jack [Nicklaus], winning 100 tournaments. The key is to see how long he can keep winning. . . . Jack did it for 25 years, but no one else has come close." — Tom Watson, whose five British Open titles include the epic head-to-head battle with Nicklaus at Turnberry in 1977

began: with Tiger Woods, a one-of-a-kind young man and that rarest of golfer who dares to be great.

Tiger's Triumphs

Major Amateur

94th U.S. Amateur, Aug. 22-28, 1994

95th U.S. Amateur, Aug. 21-27, 1995

96th U.S. Amateur, Aug. 19-25, 1996

PGA Tour

Las Vegas Invitational, Oct. 2-6, 1996

Walt Disney/Oldsmobile Classic, Oct. 17-20, 1996

Mercedes Championships, Jan. 9-12, 1997

Masters, April 10-13, 1997

GTE Byron Nelson Classic, May 15-18, 1997

Motorola Western Open, July 4-7, 1997